MW01697499

Night Hunters

Dave Luckett

Night Hunters

 Published by Scholastic Inc., 555 Broadway, New York, NY, 10012, by arrangement with Omnibus Books.
Printed in the U.S.A.

ISBN 0-439-08086-X

6 7 8 9 10 23 06 05 04

What You Should Know about *Night Hunters*

Prem is a student in the 21st century. And the schools of the future have become *extremely* interesting. During a class called Zoo, students can actually become animals.

Here's how it works. Say Prem has to learn about moles. He plugs an input cord into a small terminal that is attached to his head. The cord links to a powerful computer that connects Prem to the mind of a mole.

Prem now has all the instincts of a mole. He knows what moles like to eat and how they find food. He knows where they live and how they dig their tunnels.

He also knows which animals hunt moles and how to hide from them. That's important, because if the mole is hurt or killed—so is Prem.

For Prem, the whole experience is pretty cool. In normal life, he gets around in a wheelchair. But when he becomes an animal, he moves as well as any other member of the species.

So far, Prem has only taken these trips into animals' minds during Zoo class. But one night, Prem's friend Hobie hacks into the computer system. Hobie works out a program that will make him become one animal after another.

Prem realizes what Hobie has done and tries to stop the experiment. But the program can't be stopped. Prem and Hobie end up together in the mind of a cat. Then an owl. Then a ferret.

And they find out that these animals' lives are more dangerous than they ever could have imagined.

To Sally

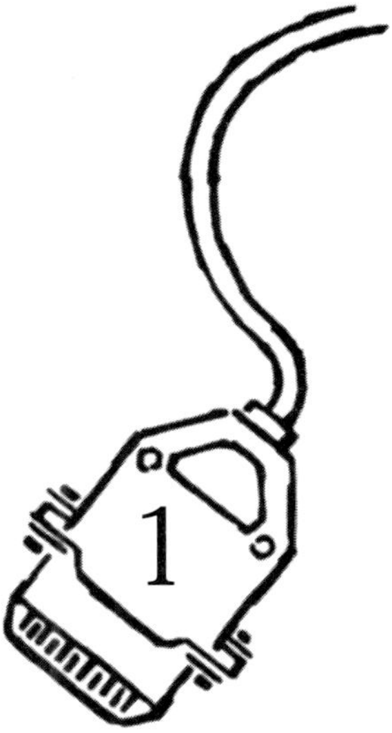

1

Thursdays at school are pretty good because the last two periods are Zoo. Animal Behavior, that is. And for a part of the time, you actually get to be an animal. Yes, sure, you have to write it all up afterward, and you have to answer all the questions, and you have to give a proof and all that. Still, it's better than being a sailor with Christopher Columbus, like we were in history class last week. Do you have any idea what sort of food those people ate? Yuck!

Not that anything really exciting ever happens in Zoo, unless you *like* being an animal. I mean, the animals they use are in controlled spaces, meaning sort of great big enclosures where they can't wander off, or get eaten. But at least it's *live.* They actually use real animals in real time, and you get to be one for a while. Not like math, where you watch graphs and tell the numbers what to do. Numbers have no feelings. Or even like history, because they use simulations for that, computer models, not real people. Zoo is better than that.

When I signed up for it, I thought it'd be even wilder than it is, though. I figured I'd be a lion, lying under a tree, thinking about my next meal, feeling all lazy and strong. Or an elephant maybe. Yeah!

But it took them half the semester to get to the first real animal. We spent that much time just getting used to being in an animal's brain, and we used simulations for that. It's just to check you out, in case there's a problem in your own mind. Like Jordan Clare, who turned out to have a fear of being closed in—what you call claustrophobia—and who had to be a mole during his second tryout.

Even when you passed that part, what you got wasn't lions or elephants. My first was a mouse. Big deal. I spent an hour hunting for seeds in a world made out of tree-sized stalks of grass and red pebbles, like it was Mars. Every now and then a shadow like a hawk's would pass over, and the mouse would freeze. It wouldn't really be a hawk, but the mouse didn't know that. And there'd be rumbles, like thunder a long way away, and you could feel the ground shake. People, walking around.

It was great, in a way. Not like being a lion, but the light was strange and everything looked different, sharp-edged, with shadows deeper than you're used to. Noises were strange, too. You could hear every creak and whistle of the wind in the grass, not a roar like a breeze in the trees but like a whole lot of sirens from miles away. And you could tell where every sound was coming from.

And the air felt thick like custard and full of scents that haven't got a name.

I spent an hour with this creature, which is as long as you're allowed, and then I had to spend another hour writing it all up. But it was worth it. I learned stuff like how a mouse hears and what it sees, and why and how its world is different from ours.

Anyway, for the rest of the semester I got to be other things. A frog, for instance. You know, they see the surface of the water they live in as a doorway between worlds. Both worlds have different rules, but both are real. And the frog lives in both. Strange, no?

And I swear it was that strangeness that hooked me. Not the feeling of living in a body with legs that work. My body works fine, generally, and I wouldn't swap having hands for anything. Or being able to talk, either. I just don't walk all that well, and generally I get around in a wheelchair. But I like strange things.

And the strangeness stayed with you, and that was good, too. Coming out of that class was weird. You'd hear the bell, and suddenly you were back in the lab. You unhook the input and take it out of the matchbox-sized terminal you've got behind your ear, the one that's actually wired into your brain. And then you'd be in class again. For a while afterward we all felt as if we should be wrinkling our noses at each other, or croaking, or whatever. It took quite a while to get used to being human again.

But anyway, I got a "B" for Zoo that term and I was really thinking I might go on with it. There are good jobs for animal partners—people who can team with a dolphin to herd fish, for example, or use a bat's sonar to count insects. So I signed up for the advanced class and that's how I met Hobie.

Hobie was twelve. He looked maybe ten, and he used to wear a T-shirt with "Boy Genius" on the front. You can ask what some twelve-year-old was doing taking advanced Zoo, and the answer was on the T-shirt. He really was. A genius, that is. Well, in a way. Mostly he was a kid though, and he had no sense, like all kids. He tried to become an animal—any animal he wanted, any time he liked. And that is crazy. Real crazy.

Maybe you haven't done Zoo, so you don't know how crazy it is. Suppose you become a dolphin, for instance. Well, that means knowing all the stuff a dolphin knows. One of the things it knows is that it can hold its breath for thirty minutes. Go ahead and try doing that. It won't work, because you're a human, and you can't. But if you're a dolphin, you think that you don't need to breathe. So you don't breathe.

So you die.

See, what I'm trying to tell you about Zoo is that you *don't* become a human in an animal's body. If you did, it would make your moves and your heartbeat and everything all wrong. No, what happens is you actually *become* the animal. The only thing you keep is your human ability to think about what you're doing, what they call higher processing. But you don't think about breathing or stuff like that at all.

So, picking the parts of your brain that you need to

take with you into the animal isn't easy. That's why it takes a *big* computer to run Zoo. Even the one at school has a hard job running the brain-to-brain interface, and that program has alarm bells and whistles in case somebody hacks into it. Because nobody—nobody—should try to step right into any animal's mind without screening. I mean, forgetting that you have to breathe is only the first thing you have to worry about. There are lots of others.

But there's Hobie, trying it. Dumb kid. Only he's smart enough to get around the protection on the computer. Smart, but dumb—if you know what I mean.

I rolled into the lab that night after wheelchair athletics, and there he was.

I was late for home and in a hurry. I remembered that I'd left my bag in the lab after class, and I was hoping I'd only find the janitors there. I figured I was lucky when I found the lights were on. Lucky nothing.

The lab is a big, clean-smelling room with a row of input jacks on a bench that runs right around the walls.

In the middle, there's a control console so that the teacher can see what everybody is doing. The actual computer is across town, and the animal control space is somewhere else again, in the real zoo maybe. But Hobie's in the lab, and he's wired into the control console in the center of the room, and he's got a mangy old alley cat in a cage, and he's tapping away on a keyboard.

"Hey, Hobie," I say. "You see my bag around? I must've left it . . ."

And then I say a really dumb thing.

"Hobie," I say, "what are you doing?"

Yeah, yeah, I know. Anybody with half a brain should have figured out what he was doing. But I was tired and it was late. I was worried about that bag, and I wasn't thinking.

He pulled the keyboard jack out and stared at me, eyes wide and not blinking.

"Hobie?" I say. "It's me, Prem."

Then it was like he snapped out of it.

"Oh, you," he says. "Um, it's extra study credit. A

special project."

Well, I didn't stop to question him. I mean, would you? But after I found my bag and headed for home, I got to thinking. What was Hobie doing, wired into the *control* console? And what was he doing with that keyboard? And the cat?!

I'm waiting for the special bus, and it hits me. No, not the bus, dummy—the answer. It's late—I mean dinner will be in the oven, and I'm hungry—I almost didn't go back. But I had to, now that I knew. Dumb kid. *Dumb* kid.

So I charged straight up the hill, into the science building, around two corners, and slammed into the lab.

And there was Hobie.

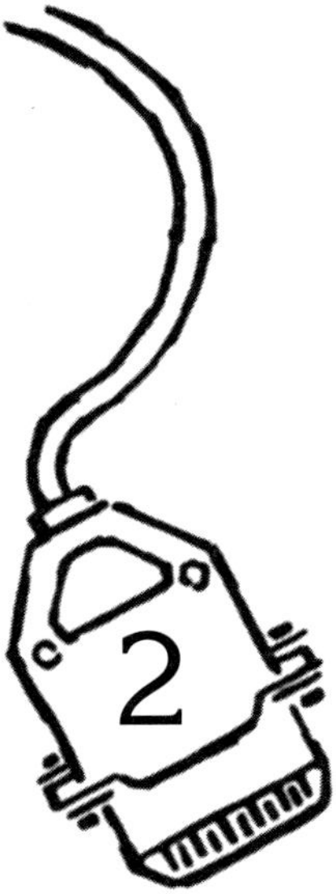

Or rather, there he *wasn't.* His body was there, but his mind was far away. Slumped into his seat, he looked like he was dead already, wired into the console. The keyboard that he had used to hack into the system was idle under his fingers, and the cat—gone.

I checked him out. He was still breathing, but it was quick and shallow, and his pulse was fast, way too fast. So I went to pull out the jack that he's got wired into his head. It was hard to reach—I had to back up and push in right next to the bench, and the wheelchair was hard to get in there—and then I stopped. There was no jack.

No jack! No simple little plug that fits into the socket in the box just behind the ear. No. A bunch of wires led from a flat case on the desk, and Hobie had hooked all of them up to contacts inside that box on his head, the one that talks to the computer. He'd actually taken the cover off of his own input and rewired it. You aren't supposed to be able to do that. He must have used a dentist's mirror and some strong glue. Dumb kid. *Dumbdumbdumb* kid. Now I couldn't just unplug him and slap him around. He was out of it, a long way out.

Time to call for help. This was crazy. The flat case on the desk was something new, too. It had what looked like at least three radios in it and a lot of other wiring I didn't understand. I reversed and headed for the door, but then Hobie stiffened and the hair on his head started to rise. And that meant trouble.

There's some feedback, of course. When your brain

is connected to an animal's, your body feels some of the things the animal's body is feeling. But this was more than "some." Hobie was breathing hard and stiffening up, and I panicked. I had to get him out of this. I reached for the master switch on the console, and flicked it off. Nothing happened. He'd shorted around it. I panicked even more.

Only one way to get him out. I'd need to talk to the computer myself. I grabbed what I thought was its input lead, and plugged it into my own head.

But what came up wasn't the workbench I was used to, and it only lasted a second. There was a ripple, and suddenly *I've become a cat.* That alley cat I saw in the lab earlier—to be precise.

And I'm looking the biggest, meanest, nastiest ginger tomcat I've ever seen, right in the eye. He's bigger than I am, and he's seriously ticked off with me. I could tell that from the way he's spitting and yowling and his fur is standing up. And there's Hobie in there, too, looking out through the same pair of eyes, enjoying it all.

"Yah!" says Hobie. "Your mother goes bow-wow!"

I suppose I could tell you what happens next like they do in the comics. You know, Blam! Wallop! Pow! Yikes! But even that isn't fast enough. That cat swipes with his right like he means to open us up like a package of potato chips, but Hobie and I lean aside and only get a scratch down one side of the face, missing our eye. But we run into his left, and that hurts. Badly. And Hobie is so surprised by this that he loses control.

I grab my chance, and the controls, at the same time. I make us run like we're being chased by packs of wolves, and I head for the nearest boundary of this guy's territory—which I know by scent, of course.

Only he's right behind us, yelling and cursing, fit to spit blue sparks, and swiping now and then at our tail and back legs. Don't believe what you hear about big, heavily built guys not being able to run fast. I'm giving it our best, but he stays right up there with us.

It's dark, but everything is clear as day, silver in the light, blue in the shadows. There are a million different scents in the air, only I don't have time to sort through them now. We hold a narrow lead through a garden, over a brick wall and into a backyard full of moving shapes of shrubs and ripples of moonlight.

We lose him for a second when we swarm up a tree, but he isn't far behind as we jump from the tree to a tool-shed roof, skim across it like a stone across a pool of silver water, drop down to a fence, then to a wheelbarrow and the ground again. There's a scent boundary here, and I know there should be another tomcat who owns the territory on the other side of it. We cross the border and crash into another bush like it was the goal line.

Only our boy behind is just too mad to care. He keeps on coming, so I have to keep on going. I pick up the feet and lay them down, come to a wall—it's too high to climb—and take a corner on two legs, straining to keep our lead. There's an opening in the wall ahead, and I charge into it. Anything to throw the chase off.

Bad move. It's the side door to an old garage, now storage for gardening tools. The front door is shut, and there's no other entrance.

It's dark, so dark that even with a cat's eyes there are shadows to hide in, and a chance that we can pass him. I duck us behind a box as he comes in the door and checks, then prowls forward. He's yelling loud threats, but that doesn't matter. If we can just get him to go past us, we can double back toward the door and maybe lose him.

Did I say we had a chance? I'd forgotten about Hobie. This is the moment he chooses to grab control, jump out from behind the box, get one shot in at the bad guy's face, and sprint for the door again. Stupid, dumb kid. Another ten seconds and we'd have caught our breath, and had a lead. As it is, the tomcat's right behind us and madder than ever. Hobie has annoyed him even more. He's screaming his head off about what he's going to do to us when he catches us.

Sheesh. And to think he probably has a name like "Twinkles" or "Muffin" when he's with humans.

Out the door and into the moonlight again. This is

no time to be steering by committee, so I don't interfere as Hobie dodges left and heads for a pile of garbage cans. At least on the top we can play king-of-the-hill. But he dodges again, jumps into a can that's lying on its side, and prepares to hold the enemy off.

Bad idea. It just proves that being bright isn't the same as being streetwise. That ginger-colored meat mincer can take us any time he wants, whether or not we protect our rear, and he knows it. He stops for maybe a second, and then he comes right up to the can, flexing and posing, and he looks in. Hobie backs up and gets ready.

Well, I figure if you have to do something, you might as well do it right. I let fall a couple of remarks about the way the enemy smells—it might get him angry enough not to know what he's doing. But he just yells right back, and then he gets ready to spring. He'll be on top of us, and after that it won't matter if the can protects our back.

He takes his time about it, too, because now he's

just playing with us. He creeps forward a little, digs his toes in. Here it comes . . .

But suddenly the tomcat that owns this patch lands on top of him like a black-and-white buzz-saw, spitting and yowling and clawing. Our boy screams, fit to take the top of your head off, and then there are two cats rolling around on the ground, a ginger one and a black-and-white one. I figure maybe the last arrival is a little smaller, but he is still putting up a good fight. I'm not staying around to umpire, though. The cavalry has arrived, and we're out of there.

Hobie doesn't argue as we run out of the can, hang a left, and head for the hills. For the rooftops, at least. We don't pause until we're half a street away and two stories up, on the flat roof of an office building. No doubt some other cat thinks it owns this piece of turf, but as long as we keep quiet, it shouldn't be a problem.

Peace, perfect peace. And now for Hobie. Only he gets in first.

"Wasn't that great? Isn't it great? And you run pretty

well, considering."

"Considering what?"

"That you, uh, don't do a lot of it."

"No, I don't. How much running on all fours do you do, kid?"

"Um. Yeah. Well, at least you won't want to get back right away."

"What do you mean by that crack?" I ask. But I know what he means. If I'm in a wheelchair, I don't want to go back to it, do I? I mean, anything—even being a cat—must be better, right?

Wrong. Well, mostly. I tell him I don't like surprises, that I do indeed want out, and that I want out right now. But he doesn't listen to the last part.

"So how'd you get into this?" he asks, and I sigh and tell him that, too.

"Oh. You mean you picked up that loose jack by mistake and plugged yourself into the system. Sorry. That's just a leftover circuit linked into this one. The whole system is just rigged together. But it works, it works. I can patent it tomorrow—it'll make me rich!"

"Rich, my foot. Listen, you dumb kid, I want out of this. *Now*, if not sooner."

"Mm? Oh. Sorry. I can't. Not right away."

"What? Why not?"

"Well, it's on a timer. I had to do a proper field trial. It's not science if you can't repeat your results, you know."

"You mean you're relying on a timer to shut the system down? No panic button?"

There's a pause. Then, "You know," he says, thoughtfully, "Maybe that would have been a good idea."

"Aaargh! You . . . you . . ." Words fail me. "Wait till I get my hands on you!"

"Oh, come on. Be reasonable. This is science. Just think of the importance."

"What importance, you crudball? What's new about this? They've been able to plug into an animal's brain for ten years now!"

"Sure they have, as long as they put a relay into the

animal's head, which means cutting it open. I've worked out a way to do it without cutting. It just sits on a collar around the neck. Works by bone conduction."

I become aware that I am wearing a collar, and there's a weight on it.

"But best of all," Hobie goes on, "I think it can be used for humans, too. Just think. No more drilling holes in people's skulls just so they can talk directly to a computer. Great, huh?"

"Terrific." I try to sound cool about it, but I had to admit it's pretty good. Still, I have other problems. "And how long before we're out of this?" I ask.

"There's half an hour on the timer."

"How long to go?"

"Not too long, I think. You know how your time sense is different when you're an animal."

"Yeah." It felt like hours already. "So let's just stay put and wait it out, okay?"

"Oh, come on. Where's your sense of adventure? The night is young."

"Listen, kid, this cat's not going anywhere. Try it and see. I can veto whatever you do, and it'll be just like the cat was having a fit."

"Hmmph. If you say so," says Hobie. He sounds scornful. I couldn't care less.

"I sure do say so."

So we wait. Hobie keeps wanting to get up and walk around, but I'm not interested in the rooftop tour. Finally, there's a sound like a gong, only I know I'm not hearing it with my ears. I sigh with relief. In a moment, I'll be back in my own skin, and free to tear Hobie limb from limb. If I can catch him.

The workbench comes up, but then it ripples again, and then I'm looking down at rooftops and streets passing below me, bright in moonlight, clearer than any human ever saw them by night.

And I'm flying.

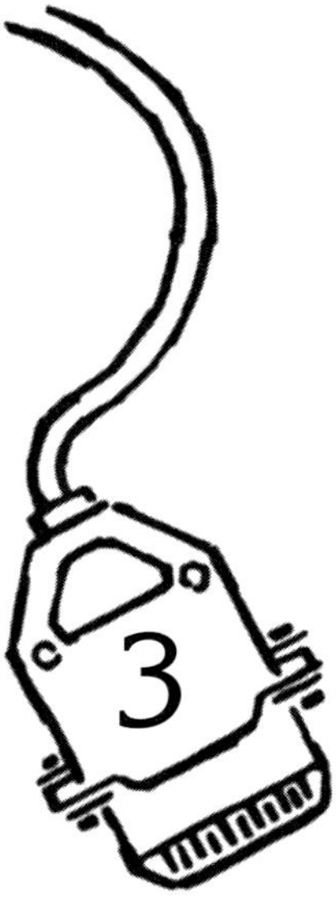

3

"You did *what*?"

"I told you. It's not science unless you can repeat your results. I had to be sure. So I wired up three animals, to try each in turn. All nighttime hunters. This is the owl. Isn't it great?"

A great truth suddenly dawns on me.

"You're crazy," I say softly, and chills go up and down my back. "I'm trapped in an owl with a mad boy-scientist."

"Aw, come on," he says. "Mad scientists went out with CDs. And you have to admit, this is brilliant!"

Well, okay, he's right. The night is brilliant, as in shining brightly. The owl's eyes are even better than the cat's, and everything glistens in the moonlight like beaten silver. Silver in a million different shades that humans can't see, or see only very badly. Roads look like strips of sheet lead, all weathered and dull, but gardens and houses range from tin-like to mirror-bright, like a forest made out of metal. The harsh spots of light from windows and street lamps actually hurt us to look at them, like they were strobes.

And the flying! Owls fly almost without any noise at all, and it's a feeling like you have this huge cushion always under you. You can't see it and you can't feel it, except it holds you up. Hobie does a loop-the-loop, just for the fun of it. For some reason, this doesn't feel so good, and suddenly I know why.

"Hobie," I say, "this owl is hungry. Really hungry. Hungry enough to pass out, maybe."

"Uh," he says, and checks. "Yeah. So he is. And I was just getting into this. Well, he can eat afterwards."

He hasn't gotten the point. "Hobie," I say gently, "did they tell you about birds in Zoo?"

"Yeah. A little, Well, I read the book. But I was in a hurry to get to the bit about how their brains work, so I might have skipped some. So what?"

I lose my temper. "So what? This is what, you dumb kid. Birds have to fly, right? And they have to keep warm at night, right? And they use up a lot of energy to do that, get it? And they can't lug a lot of body weight around. So they have to eat little and often. A human can go maybe a week without a meal. An owl has to eat every day."

"Well, I caught him last night. And there was no chance to feed him during the day. So now what?"

"Terrific. How many mouseburger stands do you see around here, dummy? None? I hope you're real good at catching them."

But Hobie is not to be put off. "I'm an owl, no?

I'm good enough."

"You hope. So quit showing off and start hunting."

We slow down and drop onto a branch in a big tree in Freeway Park, which is three blocks from the school. Ever since they banned private cars and tore up the freeways to save oil, there's been more and more wildlife creeping back into the city. So we are hoping, really hard, that dinner will come strolling past before too long. We tweak the ears and eyes up to max, and wait.

The night is full of noises, mostly human. That's the trouble with being a night hunter in a city. It's too loud.

But in the silver-bladed grass there are many small rustles and squeaks, and our owl's eyes pick up the forms of the little things that make the sounds. Most of them are bugs of one sort or another, which are not owl food mostly, but this owl is so hungry that a grasshopper or two would not go amiss. Still, I'm hoping for a mouse. Hoping?! If I were a human I'd be drooling at the thought. An owl thinking "mouse" is like a human thinking "hamburgers." I start thinking how much I'd like a big hamburger, only it all gets mixed up with how I'd like a mouse steak. This is really a weird feeling . . .

"Bandit at six o'clock!"

And Hobie throws us off the branch and we powerdive straight at the ground.

I've been daydreaming. Alright, night-dreaming. I look where Hobie's diving, and I see where the next tree trunk is, and I try to pull us up. No way. We're committed, and Hobie won't give up control anyway.

"Yahoo!" yells Hobie.

I'd close my eyes if I could, but of course that would do no good. Besides, I need to see what to do, if we're going to have a chance to get out of this.

The ground comes up far too fast. Mice are tricky little creatures. I know, I've been one—and Hobie has forgotten that the faster you go, the more effort it takes to turn. Also the more noise you make—which is why the mouse hears us coming, and dodges. Also the less time to avoid the tree trunk. Which we hit, but fortunately not straight-on. That would break our wings, and then it would be a painful wait for a cat or a fox to come by. But the hit is still worth a bruise or two.

"Ouch!" says Hobie, surprised.

I am not surprised, because I could see this coming, and I grab the chance to get control back from him. He sulks while I haul us around and try a slower, shallow dive, searching the ground underneath. The mouse has vanished, of course. Smart mouse.

"Hobie," I say, while I'm doing this, "suppose you let me fly this beast, while you keep your eyes peeled for meat. I think I'm better at missing trees."

"If you say so, Captain", says Hobie, sullenly. "You've got more experience at this, I guess." A cheap shot. Experience at missing things, he means. Like in a wheelchair, he means. I am going to have to talk to him about this; I can see that coming now.

Maybe then he got all wrapped up in his own thoughts, like I did, and he wasn't watching, because I see the next mouse about a minute later myself. I let the owl go into autopilot, and it does the rest, swooping just about right and grabbing the mouse so hard it's dead before it knows it. Luckily we came up behind it. And that's about a quarter of the day's calories right there.

I can hear you saying, "Yuck, gross!" from here. But I keep telling you, you actually *become* the animal in Zoo. That mouse is a T-bone steak with all the trimmings, as far as we're concerned.

We have two more "steak" dinners and a "cheeseburger"—Hobie finds a lizard, as well—before we feel like stopping. Luckily it's spring. If it were winter, food would be harder to find. And we do feel better.

Or do we? Feel better, that is. Have we overeaten? We feel full, somehow. Heavy. And there's a feeling as if we have forgotten to do something. Something real important.

"Uh-oh," I say. "Now what?"

"What?" says Hobie.

"I don't know," I reply, and then there's a feeling inside me and suddenly I *do* know.

"Hobie, you moron," I yell, "where did you find

this owl?"

"Right around here somewhere," he says, surprised. "Maybe a bit north, up the strip. Why?"

"Head north, then. And hope it recognizes the ground. Come on, let's go."

"Why? We've eaten already. I was going to—"

"Forget it, kid." I put some effort into getting above the trees and start pumping wings. "You'd better hope we can find this thing's nest."

"Oh, come on. It's not time to go home yet, just because we're feeling a little off. Maybe we shouldn't have had that lizard . . ."

"Lizard, schmizard," I say. "That's why we were so hungry. We're eating for two—or more."

"Huh? That's crazy. Even though there are two of us, we're still only one owl."

"Guess again, boy wonder." I spot what I'm looking for—a hollow in a tree, familiar somehow. "We're about to become a mother."

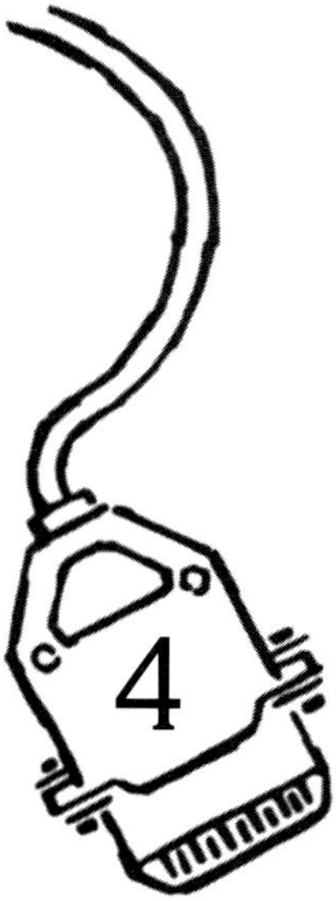

4

I bet you think that birds' nests are sort of like a house—all comfy and with a place to sit down and all. Uh-uh. They're built out of twigs and moss and down, and they're in the hollow of a tree. The twigs are sharp, and they stick into tender parts of you, especially when you're laying an egg. Trust me on this.

Also, the moss is damp, and the whole thing doesn't smell so good. And they're alive with fleas, and worse.

A home away from home it isn't.

Owls don't do the hot water and clean sheets bit when they go into labor, either, which is just as well, because there's nobody to rush around getting them anyway. But I'll say one thing for laying eggs—it's quicker and easier than what humans do. Sort of like the difference between making dinner and sending out for pizza. Still, I'm glad when it's over.

So is Hobie. Only he thinks the whole thing is truly gross, and wants to leave the nest immediately. "Forget it," I say. "You got this owl into this, and you can let her continue with raising her family without bothering her further. We stay right here."

"I want to go flying."

"Well, you can't. The eggs will get cold. Shut up and wait."

If Hobie had a lip to stick out, he'd stick it out. Dumb kid. But I'm not turning over control to him. We wait.

Fine. Only Hobie decides to needle me about it.

"I guess you have to be cautious, what with your . . .

problem and all."

"What's that supposed to mean?"

"Well . . . being, like, disadvantaged, uh, you have to be careful . . ."

Disadvantaged. I'd come apart if I got pushed, he thinks. Dumb kid.

I sigh. "No, I don't have to be careful. I just don't have to act like a danger freak. Nobody does—not even you."

"Oh, come on. Don't you ever get tired of being careful all the time? Wouldn't you just once like to take a jump into the—"

The gong sounds in my ears. Yay! We're out of this!

The workbench comes up, rippling, then goes to black. Pitch black.

". . . dark? . . ."

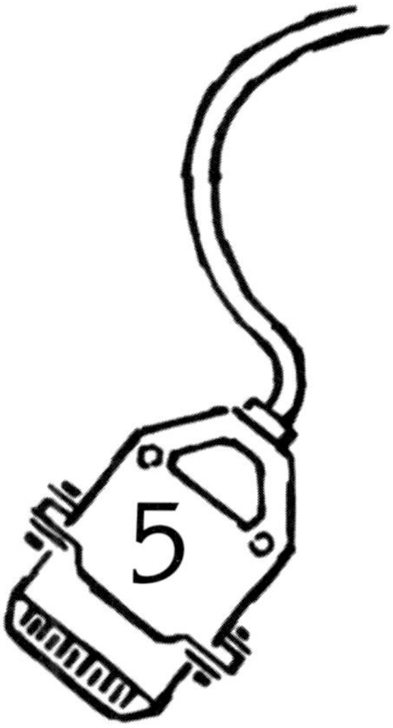

5

"Like this, you mean?"

Hobie doesn't say anything. He's checking it out. So am I.

All around us there are the rough scents of earth and plant roots and the cool feel of dirt. We're underground. And there are other smells, musky rabbit and another one—cold, like the feel of metal—that sets alarm bells ringing in my head, but I don't know why.

I move us a little from side to side, lift the head a bit. It's a tight squeeze, so tight that I can't work our front paws up alongside our head, but I feel tunnel walls. The tunnel is the same shape as we are, like a tube. Our whiskers tell us about the walls, which are rough and pebbly, and something in our head is telling us that we are heading down. Down. Suddenly I don't want to go on down. Only there's no space to turn around. The tunnel is just a little wider than we are, and though our body feels flexible and limber, it's long. Too long. We're shaped like a dachshund. What is this?

"Hobie," I say, "just what are we now?"

"Uh," he says. "It's a ferret. You know, one of those long, skinny things."

"I know what a ferret is. What's it doing down some burrow?"

"How would I know? Going down holes is just what ferrets do, I guess."

"Let's not go along with it. I think we should back up and get out of here."

Hobie starts to object, and then decides not to.

"Yeah. Maybe you're right. There's something not quite right about this."

He sounds a little quiet, and that pleases me. Could it be that Hobie's scared of the dark?

So anyway, we scramble for footing and begin to reverse, but it's difficult. The tunnel is quite steep, and our fur is all the wrong way. Worse, the collar around our neck is tight, and it keeps snagging on roots and stuff that hang from the roof and come out of the wall. And our movement makes noise. Suddenly, somehow, I don't think it's a good idea to make noise.

"Hold it a minute," I whisper, which is crazy, since only Hobie can hear what I say. This is like the ferret is thinking to itself, after all.

But Hobie stops, and I stop, and the ferret stops, and we listen to the dark, and try to figure out the scents and the other feelings we get from the whiskers.

It's pitch black, and it's hard to explain how black that is. There's no light at all. No matter how good your eyes are, no matter how long they have to get used to the dark, you can't see anything with no light at all. The ferret's got pretty good eyes, but there's nothing to see but black, black like it only gets when you're underground. But the ferret's also got pretty good ears, a good nose, and long whiskers. The whiskers are like eyes, and they're able to build up a picture of the tunnel around us.

I guess it was the smell of a rabbit that brought him in here in the first place. He's hungry, for the same reason that the owl was hungry, and there *have* been rabbits in here. This is a warren, then. But the scent is cold. An old warren, maybe one that's not used any more, because I don't smell rabbit so much now. What I smell is cold, like metal. A trap? The scent's got a musky sort of overlay to it, and it smells alive . . .

And then there's a sound in the dark ahead of us, maybe a couple of body-lengths away. A dry scraping, with a harsh squeak over the top of it which we wouldn't have heard with human ears. And there's a pressure of air movement on our whiskers, just a fleeting one.

Something has moved in the tunnel ahead of us. Something dry and hard—with scales, not fur. Something long, like a tube, like us.

Snake. It's a snake!

It's like I've swallowed a bunch of safety pins, and they've all opened up at once inside me. We're held motionless, face-first, with nothing between us and the enemy but a set of whiskers. And it's dark, black like the end of the world in a coal mine.

Has Hobie figured it out? I check him. He's mute, and back in the lab his body would be shivering and sweating bullets. He's figured it out, alright. The snake moves again in the dark, and our whiskers are so tuned to the air movement that we can feel the tiny quiver as its tongue flickers in and out. It must be close enough to sense our body heat. They can do that.

Panic is starting to rise. If we move, we won't hear anything over the noise we make, and we'll be telling the snake exactly where we are. If we don't, the snake will just sit there until it knows anyway, and then it'll strike.

Hobie begins to wail, and would start to scramble backward if I'd let him.

"Shut up! Stop moving, Hobie, right now! Cool it!"

"It's a snake, you moron. If it bites us, we're dead meat."

"We move, and we'll be telling it where to bite. Stay still. Shut up. It's not sure, yet."

"I . . . I can't stand snakes . . ." The last word is shaky, panicky.

"It has to pull back to strike. If we stay still, we'll feel it coming. It has to push air ahead of it in the tunnel . . ."

I try to speak calmly, easy, like I know what I'm doing. But Hobie isn't hearing very well.

"But it'll bite us—"

"Only if it hits. We can duck . . ." But there is no answer. Hobie has gone into shock.

Well, as long as he's not going to interfere. I go back

to listening and feeling the air with the whiskers, not moving, trying to act like a stone. Maybe we can fake the snake out. They usually don't like tangling with things that bite back, and after all, he's only got one shot.

It's a pretty good shot, though.

I try to remember what I know about snakes, and yeah, sure, they often use a rabbit burrow as a den. After they've cleaned the rabbit out of it, that is. But a lot of snakes don't have poison. Carpet snakes, for instance. Maybe this one is like that. Or maybe he's just trying to figure out whether we're small enough to swallow, and will go away if we aren't.

On the other hand, maybe not. After all, we're in his living room here.

The snake isn't as smart as we are. He moves again in the darkness, coming closer, and now I'm almost sure of his position. I twitch the whiskers fully forward, to feel the air ahead of us.

The tunnel curves in all directions, and that's just as well. If he's going to strike, he has to do it in a curve, and that's going to slow him up. And now I'm fairly sure he's going to strike. The air goes still, dead still, and then there's a slight outward feeling in it, as though he's pulled his head back.

Hobie whimpers. I can't give him any attention just now. I just have to hope that he stays out of it.

A flicker of air along the tunnel, pushed out in front of the snake's head. Fast, and if I had a human's reflexes, I'd be a gone goose. But I have time to duck. Our face slams hard into the dirt, and the strike passes over our head and doesn't quite hit with enough force to get through the thick fur on our low-slung shoulders.

It didn't hit when the snake thought it would, either, and so it had to extend too far. And now our whiskers are in contact with the snake's head and they tell me all I need to know.

Ferrets have a mouthful of needle-sharp teeth. I snap upward, pushing off the wall, grabbing a piece of scaly throat just below the angle of the jaw, and I hang on.

It tries to pull back, tries to angle down for a strike

at our back, but it can't get a hold. It shakes its head and there's a spray of liquid on our back. Great. If I didn't know it was poisonous before, I do now. I grip and try to stay cool. If I hang on long enough, I'll choke it, or maybe there's a chance of tearing it open. But not much of a chance. This is like biting on a venetian blind. It starts to haul us forward as it pulls back, and I work the teeth harder. Now there's cold blood in our mouth.

But it's strong. Very strong, and it's got more traction than we have. But if I let go, it'll be back, and it won't miss twice, now that it knows our shape. We're being dragged, though, and we don't know what else is ahead there in the black. I scramble against the floor and walls and shake our head, tugging away. If I can just hurt it enough, it won't be able to strike again . . .

Oh, no, the tunnel's opening up. The walls and floor are getting further apart. I pull as hard as we can, but we're being drawn bit by bit into a wider chamber, the rabbit's living room. And when it's got some room, this guy will be a lot more of a problem. It might be able to

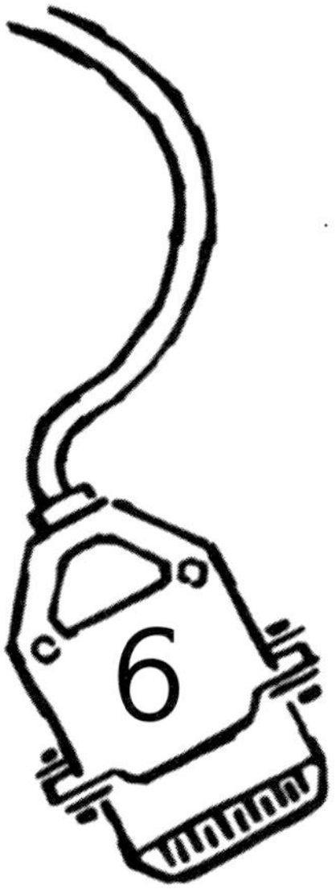

That's what does it, eventually. From then on, the snake is mainly trying to get away, and we rip in harder, and start to gouge out chunks. Eventually the struggling starts to slow down, and the snake ripples and jerks, rather than slinging us from side to side. Some time after that, we realize that it's doing it from memory, and we let go so it can get on with it.

It takes what seems an awfully long time to die.

We lean against the cold earth and wait for the thunder of our heart to die down.

Hobie, for once, hasn't got anything to say. Neither have I. We just wait there in the dark and listen to the snake dying, thinking about how it could've been us. That goes on for some time.

"Um," says Hobie, at last.

"Yeah," I say. "You were right. I forgot. I was under pressure, and I forgot . . ."

"No," says Hobie, breaking in. "I have to say I'm sorry. Sorry for yelling at you."

"What? Oh, that. You didn't mean it."

"Still, I'm sorry. And I was the one who came apart when it got difficult. I was scared."

"You and me both. We were both scared."

"You didn't act scared."

"There's more than one style of being scared. One style is doing crazy things to prove to yourself that you're not scared."

Hobie chewed on that idea a while. Then, "And I got

The Author

Dave Luckett was born in Sydney, Australia, but has lived most of his life in Perth, Australia. He discovered science fiction at the age of thirteen, and, he says, has "never been weaned away from it since." As a writer, his chosen fields are science fiction and fantasy. Dave has had short stories published in the SF magazine *Eidolon*, and in 1994 his story "The Patternmaker" was published in Omnibus Books' science fiction anthology of the same name. He has also published a book for younger readers, *The Adventures of Addam*.